My Life as a Mustard Seed
by Beth Armstrong

"Sometimes when you're in a dark place you think you've been buried, but actually you've been planted."

-Tony Evans

"For a seed to achieve its greatest expression, it must come completely undone. The shell cracks, its insides come out and everything changes. To someone who doesn't understand growth, it would look like complete destruction."

-Cynthia Occelli

Preface:

Have you ever wondered: Is this really all there is to my life? Is this what I was really created for/to do? Is life really meant to just be about going through the motions, checking boxes, and being 'responsible'? If so, then the **Growing Roots for a Mission Driven Life** series is for you!

Growing Roots for a Mission Driven Life is a 7-day devotional series designed to help you discover God's purpose & unique calling for your life. Through this devotional series, you'll identify the steps needed to uncover your unique 'seed' or calling from Christ; learn the importance of planting yourself in the church to your calling; craft a personalized mission statement for your life which will assist you in identifying goals and priorities needed to successfully live out your calling; reveal your specific calling by discovering your spiritual gifts and strengths; produce actionable steps to nourish your seed for future growth, and more.

We'll spend our time diving into Biblical examples and learning what the Bible says regarding the impact of our daily decisions.

Colossians 2:7 "Let your roots grow down into him, and let your lives be built on him. Then your faith will grow strong in the truth you were taught, and you will overflow with thankfulness."

About the Author:

Rooted Leaders founder, Beth Armstrong, is a Waco native and Baylor alumna. She continues to reside in Waco today with her husband of 17 years and has been blessed to raise her children Hunter and Ella.

In 1998, fresh out of college, I began my career as an English teacher with the idea of my calling to impact the lives of the students I met. I loved being able to immerse into the material and help the students find their own 'aha' moment. After 4 years, I realized that while the calling to serve others was correct, the profession was not.

Shortly after leaving the field of education, I began a career in the pharmaceutical industry. It was here that I was introduced to thought leaders such as Marcus Buckingham, John Maxwell, Rick Warren and many more. During my 14 years in the sales world, my desire to learn more about leadership development and strength building began. As I learned more about the importance of living a life built on your natural strengths, I began to share my excitement and key learnings with fellow teammates to help them grow and bloom in their own careers.

It was during this time in pharmaceutical sales that I began volunteering with the Junior League of Waco: a nonprofit organization for women committed to promoting voluntarism, developing the potential of women, and improving the community through the effective action and leadership of trained volunteers. After 14 years of active service and concluding as the President of this organization, I began to believe so strongly in the importance of developing the potential in EVERY woman.

In 2016, I began looking for opportunities to expand my love of developing the potential in women to help them find their unique calling and launched Rooted Leaders in 2017. Looking back, the journey for creating Rooted Leaders, dates back almost 20 years. I am more convinced than ever of the great need for women's leadership development as well as the need for women lifting up other women as we help each other uncover the purpose God has planned for our life.

I feel humbled to have the opportunity to help other women find their calling and live the life God created them to lead through this company. As a mom, I can think of no better legacy to leave my children than a lifetime of serving others.

Thank you for going on this journey with me,

–Beth

Get to Know *Beth Armstrong* and her work through *Rooted Leaders* at:
www.rootedleaders.org
or follow Rooted Leaders on Social Media

About Rooted Leaders:

All great leaders have deep roots that they rely on to sustain them and support them when they're leading others-especially during the difficult times. Just like in the Bible, the characters that we know so well teach us that their own roots developed deep in the soil of God. It is only through growing our own roots deep into who God is and uncovering who He made us to be that we, too, will lead the life He created for us. Once we have begun this transformational process and begin to apply proven leadership principles, can we bear abundant fruit and live the life we never dreamed possible.

Table of Contents:

Day 1: We ALL have a Seed

Day 2: Seed Germination

Day 3: The Importance of Being Planted

Day 4: The Culling Process: How Compacted is My Soil?

Day 5: Satan's Herbicide

Day 6: Root Growth; It Happens in the Dark

Day 7: Seeking God's Voice

Life as a Mustard Seed

Day 1: We ALL Have a Seed

I have a friend that lives on the west coast whom I haven't seen in person since the birth of our oldest children, but whenever we talk our conversation always starts mid-sentence regardless if we've talked daily or not in months. Without fail, one of us will pick up the phone and begin as if we've been talking for hours, "so I was at the store earlier today, and…" it's this wonderful familiarity that allows our relationship to grow through easy days and difficult ones. We have a mutual understanding that we both have each other's best interest at heart, regardless of the topic at hand.

So, my new friend, that's how I would like to begin our time together. Almost mid-sentence with you knowing, however difficult the material may be for you, I have your very best interest at heart. Please know that I am praying, right now, as I write these words that God would use this devotional series to encourage you, challenge you, strengthen you in your walk and in your desire to seek his will for your life.

Whether you are reading this devotional series as a 16, 26, 46, 66, or 96-year-old, I want to start by saying YOU.ARE. SPECIAL. I don't know when the last time was that someone told you that, but I want you to know that I know and God knows that YOU.ARE.SPECIAL.

Regardless of your current situation, whatever your life looks like right now, YOU were created ON PURPOSE FOR a PURPOSE. Whether your parents intended you to be born or not, GOD created you and equipped you with a special calling. You, my sweet friend, are not an accident. How am I special, you may ask?

Psalm 139:13 "For you created my inmost being; you knit me together in my mother's womb. I praise you because I am fearfully and wonderfully made; your works are wonderful, I know that full well."

Jeremiah 29:11 "For I know the plans I have for you,' declares the Lord, 'plans to prosper you and not to harm you, plans to give you hope and a future."

The God of the universe, in his infinite wisdom, *KNEW* that he wanted *YOU* to be born exactly how you were, when you were and where you were. He was the one who hand-picked every detail and characteristic about you-even the ones you don't like. He knew exactly what you needed to develop a heart of service towards him and others, and he knew exactly the people you would intersect with throughout your life that would need YOU to bring his light into their life. Whether your childhood was filled with love and laughter or abuse and neglect, God has a GOOD plan designed for your life. He has a plan that can redeem anything you have walked through. A plan designed not to harm you, but to give you a hope and a future. A plan that will open opportunities for you to share your experience of God through the unique lens of your life.

As God was knitting you together in your mother's womb, he planted a unique seed or calling on your life. Because of that seed, YOU, are so special to him. The God of the universe sees EVERYTHING you have walked through and longs for you to allow him to grow your unique seed so that you, too, can witness the specialness of the fruit your life will bear.

God, in his infinite wisdom, knew that identifying his calling on our life could be unclear and surrounded us with tangible examples to help us grasp and concretely understand his plan for our life. Thankfully for us, God utilizes the process he created for seed development in nature to give us clear patterns and explanations of our own spiritual growth and development. My hope is that you will begin to see God's direction for your life mirrored through nature's processes as well.

In this devotional series, we'll focus consistently on how you can grow your roots so that you live a **MISSION DRIVEN LIFE** for Christ!

John 15:16 "You have not chosen Me, but I have chosen you, and I have appointed you {I have planted in you}, that you might go & bear fruit and keep on bearing, and that your fruit may be lasting so that whatever you ask the Father in My name, He may give it to you."

Points to Ponder:

- What seed/calling has God planted in my life?
- What is unique or special about me that God could use to lead others to him?
- What do the following verses mean for my life? 2 Timothy 1:9, 1 Corinthians 1:9, Psalm 37:23-24

Life as a Mustard Seed

Day 2: Seed Germination

I must admit, I'm thrilled you're still hanging with me after day 1. I hope you're starting to get as excited as I do now about how cool our God is to utilize the nature he created all around us in teaching us more about Him and His role in our life.

Now, that you've been introduced to the idea of God planting a 'seed' or a calling in you, let's delve into how God grows our seed into a mature life that bears fruit. Flipping through the Bible, there are over 300 references to plants, nature, seeds, roots, etc. If God refers to plant life that many times, that's a sign to me there's a correlation or a process he wants us to understand.

With this theme of nature in mind, let's chat for a minute about the awesomeness of the mustard seed. (Who doesn't love a good mustard seed?!) What I love about God, is that out of ALL the seeds he created and could have referenced, he chose one of the smallest and potentially most insignificant seeds to draw our attention to. There are days where I can identify with the mustard seed. Days where all I see is my outward smallness or my circumstances. Days where I feel insignificant and unqualified for God to use in any meaningful capacity. But that's EXACTLY who God often chooses to reveal his greatness and power to others.

Back to our friend the mustard seed, it measures a whopping 1-2 millimeters. In Matthew 17:20, Jesus references the amount of faith we need to that of a mustard seed, specifically, because a black mustard seed would have been the smallest known seed to local Palestinian farmers in the 1st century. The fascinating part about our friend, the seed, is that under the right conditions, this speck can create deep roots that will nourish and grow one of the largest known garden plants, reaching 20-30' tall. Who knew a mustard seed could be so cool?! There is one point I want you to remember. From the humble beginnings of a millimeter in size to a giant bush of over 30' tall, requires this seed to go through a development process which takes time; lots of time. Uncovering our seed, God's calling on our life, is no different.

On the inside cover of this book, I quoted Cynthia Occelli who said,

> "For a seed to achieve its greatest expression, it must come completely undone. The shell cracks, its insides come out and everything changes. To someone

who doesn't understand growth, it would look like complete destruction."

But isn't that the way God works sometimes? He rarely changes us the way we might wish-the neat and easy way. Instead, it often requires our stubborn ways and hard hearts to be tilled by sharp blades, breaking up the hard, crusty soil of our lives removing unwanted weeds and boulders buried deep in the ground so that our seed has the room necessary to finally germinate and sprout new growth through the producing of a root.

Knowing the seed God has planted within us is important not only for proper growth to happen, but for the future harvest we will reap and then replant and reap again as we build a legacy for the generations that follow us. With the realization that when we commit to plant ourselves in good soil, allowing our hearts to be cultivated so that deep roots can grow, and that our decisions today impact more than just our future, the next step is to focus on knowing what unique calling God has given to us-what kind of seed He has planted within us.

Let's return to our botany lessons for a minute.

The process of a seed growing into a plant is called germination. (I'm not going to lie, there are days, I wish we had a term to call our transformational growth too.) For seeds to properly germinate, there are a few basic conditions that are needed. Initially, it's all about the environmental conditions when the seed is planted. Are you holding up that mirror? If not, you should be because the same can be true for us. If we want the seed God planted in us to grow, it's all about our environmental conditions too.

The first condition to determine new growth for our little seedling is how deeply it has been planted in the soil. For this new seed to sprout life, it must first be planted, hidden under the dirt-seemingly vanished from the naked eye. Because God is a God of order and processes, it's common to see him give us example after example of new growth being 'buried' or hidden in the beginning. Whether God is growing something new, such as a baby, or a new plant, or a new calling, he replicates the process of being buried, unseen from anyone else, but him, for a period.

Next, what is then produced is its most important life-sustaining system: for a plant, a root; for a baby, the brain, spinal cord, and neurological system; for a new calling, our relationship with God. Here's the tricky part. For us humans seeking God's calling on our lives, if we're not intentionally making the time to develop this life-sustaining connection to Christ, we'll never move past our 'buried seed' stage.

I don't know about you, but I started getting excited as I began to initially make connections to how God operates in nature and replicates the same process in my own life.

Returning to our new favorite botany topic, let's focus next on what's necessary for roots to grow. Root development comes down to 4 basic things:

- Water
- Oxygen
- Right Temperature
- Soil Compaction-low enough to allow for root penetration

If all the needs are met, then, the first sign of life is the growing of the roots.

Points to Ponder:

- Is my 'seed' currently planted and still in the germination phase?
- Am I growing my 'life-sustaining' roots in Christ so that He can germinate my seed?
- What does the Bible say about this in Colossians 2:7, Jeremiah 29:11, Isaiah 43:19?

Life as a Mustard Seed
Day 3: The Importance of Being Planted

For a seed to sprout to life, whether it's our little friend the mustard seed or the seed of our calling in Christ, it must first be planted. Regarding our own growth, there are two simple steps we can take today. The first and most important one is to SEEK HIM. Daily. Consistently. Diligently. Seek Him.

Jeremiah 29:13 says, "Then you will seek Me, inquire for and find Me when you search for Me with all your heart."

If you want to know God's plans for your life, then you must seek Him. There's nothing fancy or difficult about it. But, it is a command and a requirement if we want to grow into the person God has created us to be.

The second step is to make sure we are planting ourselves, where we are, right now. Being planted, allows the necessary preparation and growth to take place for our roots to grow and our calling to be found. One important distinction to make is that being planted in Christ is **NOT** just attending church. It's asking for a need or a place we can serve and be involved *while* we seek God's will and our next step. Planting ourselves provides the opportunity for:

- our gifts to be used for a greater purpose beyond ourselves
- we begin to serve "we" instead of "me"
- learn to put others first

God often requires us to give first what we want to receive; to be willing to pay for what we pray for.

In **1 Kings 18,** we read the story of a three-year drought taking place in Israel.

Here's a brief recap:

In the third year, God comes to Elijah and tells him to go to King Ahab and his prophets of Baal and tell them to prepare for rain. When Elijah meets with King Ahab, he tells the king that he cannot continue to ignore the commandments of the Lord and follow Baal. Elijah basically tells the king and the 450 prophets of Baal that God is ready for a sudden death match showdown. He asks that all the people along with the prophets go up to Mount Carmel where each side will build an altar to their god, sacrifice a bull, but not light the altar. Then, whichever god brings the fire is the one, true god. After an all-day struggle for the prophets of Baal trying to get their god to light their BBQ, Elijah says-my turn. He collects the wood while the people watch and repairs the altar while the people watch. He kills and prepares the bull while the people continue to only watch. He digs the trench around the altar, again, while the people just watch. He picks up the 12 stones and places them around the altar while the people sit idly by as spectators. Finally, Elijah requires the people to stop being spectators and start being participants. To be willing to PAY for what they had been PRAYING for. Remember, they're living in the middle of a 3-year drought so water is in very short supply. They've walked a good way away from their homes up to Mount Carmel so they only have limited access to water to begin with. Elijah comes to them towards the end of a very long day and says,

> *"(v 33b) Fill four jars with water and pour it on the burnt offering and the wood."*

Basically, he's asking them to take the VERY thing that they're praying for (water in the form of rain) and to pay it forward-to give it to God. After the people go from person to person and collect enough to fill 4 jars, Elijah instructs them to pour it out on the altar-to sacrifice it. After they do so, he tells them to do it again. Find any water left, collect it, and sacrifice it, again. Three times they go through this process.

God often requires us to stop being spectators (to PLANT ourselves) and to trust Him by becoming participants before he'll open the doors to our miracles and blessings. It wasn't until AFTER they had sacrificed what was most precious to them that the fire came, the offering burned, and God brought the rain.

If you're willing to seek God, be prepared for God to ask you to plant yourself and give first what you're wanting to receive. In doing so, you will learn more about the nature of God and who He has created you to be than you ever thought possible.

Planting yourself and allowing God to produce roots in you, will also allow you to have the support structure needed during stormy times in life. Through the planting process, you'll grow in your depth of wisdom which will be needed to make decisions about what to do and where to go. It will also allow your seed to grow so that it can provide shade for others growing under you.

Why do I need to be 'planted' first before my roots will grow?

I'm sure you've heard the adage, "bloom where you are planted." If you are asking God to use your life, to give you direction, then understand that he often starts with where you are right now and with what you already have in your hand.

Because God often gets what's in our heart into the world through what's already in our hands, it is important that we trust the same God who PLANTED the seed to OPEN the door. Until He does, we must remain planted and not make the mistake of rushing ahead of God in the excitement of our newly discovered seed. If we move too soon, before we're ready, before our roots are developed to sustain us, we will ultimately fail and bear no fruit

Jeremiah 1:5 "Before I formed you in the womb I knew you, before you were born I set you apart; I appointed you as a prophet to the nations."

Even though God chose Jeremiah to be a prophet before he was even born, Jeremiah struggled and suffered in his home town of Anathoth. Anathoth was a small and obscure town, not unlike my own. Yet even here, God saw Jeremiah and called him to do mighty works.

Jeremiah questioned God that if God had this BIG plan for him, then why was Jeremiah still in Anathoth and struggling? Why was no one listening? Jeremiah had identified his seed and planted it in Anathoth but wasn't seeing any growth or fruit. Speaking from my own experience, I know EXACTLY how Jeremiah felt and appreciate God's kindness in his answer even more!

Jeremiah 12:5 "The Lord rebukes Jeremiah for his impatience, saying 'If you have raced with men on foot and they have tired you out, then how can you compete with horses? If you fall down in a land of peace (where you feel secured), then how will you do (among the lions) in the thicket beside the Jordan?"

Basically, God is telling Jeremiah he's not ready yet. If your roots aren't sustaining you where you are currently planted at home, where it's the easiest and where you have the most support, then how can you be expected to bloom somewhere else?

Points to Ponder:

- When God does something big, He often uses small things. What small thing in my life could God be growing into something big for his kingdom?
- Where can I plant myself specifically now so that I can grow my roots deeper?
- Ministry that is effective always begins at home. How does this impact my current view for what I'm asking God to do in my life?
- Read Nehemiah 1-2. Where was Nehemiah when God planted a dream on his heart? How did Nehemiah continue to remain planted? How did God bless his obedience?

Life as a Mustard Seed

Day 4: The Culling Process-How Compacted is My Soil?

How are you feeling so far about your seed? Are you ready to begin planting your seed so that you can watch God grow it?

Regardless of whether your chomping at the bit to plant yourself or beginning to feel disheartened over the idea of not having enough time or energy to be planted, today's devotional is for you and one that you can't skip if you want to bear fruit.

Let's revisit, our initial botany lesson for a moment. You'll recall that for any seed to grow, it needs to be planted in low compacted soil. If the soil is too compacted, meaning if it's too dense and not porous enough, then the seed will never be able to receive the nutrients it needs to grow. If the soil is too compact, water & oxygen won't be able to penetrate the soil which means the seed will never germinate so root development will not take place and the plant will remain dormant.

With soil compaction being important to growth, most farmers will spend time BEFORE they plant to prepare the soil. They'll till the ground to break up large clumps of dirt and allow it to become aerated. They'll remove large boulders or weeds that may choke out the new growth. The farmer takes the time to intentionally work the soil to ensure that the seed, once planted, can grow healthy roots, and produce fruit.

Since God has mirrored the growing process of a plant to our own spiritual growth, I believe that each of us need to go through a 'culling' phase or a 'tilling' of our life before we plant ourselves in our calling.

How do I 'cull' my life?

Before you begin this process, think about who it is that prepares the ground, plants the seed, and nourishes it in nature. It's the farmer. For us to 'cull' our life so that our seed can grow, we must look to our, 'heavenly farmer'. Because he is the one who CREATED us and knows the type of seed we are, he is the one whose wisdom we need to seek regarding what in our life will lead to our seed thriving and what will lead to it remaining dormant.

For me, it means humbling myself before God and asking him to reveal to me anything and everything that doesn't need to be in my life. It means CONSISTENTLY making time to pray and to listen to whatever God shows me. It means saying no to a lot of things that I normally would have said yes to. It means culling out bad attitudes and habits and to take an honest assessment of my choices and ask God to reveal to me those things which are not bearing good fruit.

While letting go of things that I've allowed to become a part of me is a difficult journey, it's necessary if I'm serious about wanting God's best for my life. I must choose to let go and lay down difficult things now so that I begin to allow room in my compacted life for God to grow my roots. My best piece of advice as you begin your culling process is to get comfortable with being uncomfortable!

> Mitchell Baker said, "I've learned that for many people, change is uncomfortable. Maybe they want to go through it, and they can see the benefit of it, but at a gut level, change is uncomfortable."

Visualize for a minute the actual physical process involved in a planted seed sprouting roots or the tilling of soil. For the seed, the outer shell of the seed must physically break away before the root can begin to grow. For the soil to be tilled, sharp blades must penetrate the surface and break it apart. Nothing about this process in nature is easy nor comfortable. Yet, it is completely necessary before new life can begin.

Being uncomfortable will push you further than you've ever been. It will give you a reason to move on, and it will show you a wide range of new experiences. It will make you stronger and provide you with the tools necessary for you to succeed while creating opportunities to choose your direction.

Wanting to remain comfortable is natural, but no growth will take place while you remain so. If you REALLY want to grow and uncover the calling Christ has placed on your life, then you must get comfortable with being uncomfortable.

Points to Ponder:

- Pray and ask God to begin to show you places in your life where your soil is too compacted.
- Ask God to reveal any choices, attitudes, habits that are preventing you from growing your roots.
- Read James 1:5, Proverbs 2:6, Ephesians 1:17, and Psalm 51:6 What do these verses say God will grant you if you ask? How can you use this information to lower the compaction in your life?

Life as a Mustard Seed
Day 5: Satan's Herbicide

Before we wrap up our focus on planting our seed so that it can grow deep roots, it's important to identify the number one killer of our seed beyond a highly compacted soil or life. As we concluded in the last devotional, the devil works VERY hard to keep us all busy so that we don't have time for God. He is very good at utilizing what's already in our hands to distract us. Maybe for you it's the 'need' to have some downtime and watch a show on tv, scroll through *Facebook*, or play games on your phone like *Candy Crush*? Maybe, it's the internal drive to get everything on your 'to do' list accomplished like folding laundry, washing the dishes, or baking cupcakes for your child's school? Whatever tool he's using, he'll work very hard to distract you and wear you down by creating havoc and chaos in your life so that you don't have time to spend it with God.

I first heard the term, 'panem et circenses' in Levi Lusko's book, Through the Eyes of a Lion[1]. In it, he explains that "He (Satan) has to check with God before he can wreak havoc in your life, but you can do great damage to your calling without getting approval from anyone." Lusko goes on to explain that Satan is very good at keeping us occupied through a strategy called, 'panem et circenses.' It translates to 'bread and circuses'. The basic premise is that during the Roman days, the emperors realized that if people weren't bored or hungry, their freedom could be stolen. This is Satan's favorite herbicide to prevent our young seed from growing. If he can distract us; he can destroy us. Here's the catch, the distraction is difficult to detect when it's happening because it doesn't involve bad things but good things. However, it's these 'good things' that take the place of the most important things. This is why tiling our lives and lowering our level of compaction is so important. It's pivotal for our root growth to have the necessary room to stay connected, daily to God.

Satan's goal is to occupy our focus and energy with the trivial so that we spend our life focused on the superficial. If he can do this, he can keep us from our calling and deprive us of our destiny. If our "attention is diverted until [we] are dead, he will be able to get [us] to do to [ourselves] what he doesn't have the power to do to [us]."

As if the decision to let go of things we've always done wasn't hard enough, Satan will work VERY hard to make it feel like it's not 'worth the sacrifice.' NOTHING could be farther from the truth! I tell you this now, so that you'll be prepared when it happens, because it WILL happen. He might wait until your awake in the middle of the night and your guard is down or until you have an especially difficult day at work or with your spouse.

Hear me. Once you know to expect it, you can arm yourself with God's promises and SQUELCH those thoughts! Rely on the God who is ALREADY in your tomorrow; the God that knows ALL your burdens and struggles, that he has it ALL under control.

> **Isaiah 41:10** "Fear not, for I am with you. Be not dismayed, for I am your God. I will strengthen you. Yes, I will help you. I will uphold you with my righteous right hand."

Points to Ponder:

- What in my life could Satan be using as 'Bread & Circuses' to distract me from my calling?
- What are 3 things I need to STOP doing today that will help cull my soil and create space for God to grow my seed?
- How can these verses prepare me when Satan comes to wreak havoc in my life? Proverbs 3:5-6, Psalm 9:9, Psalm 86:7, John 14:1, John 14:27, and Exodus 14:14

Life as a Mustard Seed
Day 6: Root Growth; It Happens in the Dark

The fruit you see above ground is determined by what's hidden underground. It's the unseen development that has happened overtime by the roots that governs the growth above ground that others see. The bigger and healthier the root system, the bigger and healthier the plant. The same is true for our spiritual growth and the potential impact of our calling.

On Day 2, we talked about everything in life, when first starting, happens in the 'dark'. Whether we're referencing the inception of a new baby, the germination of a seed, or the activation of a calling, it all begins out of sight, hidden from everyone but the creator. The hard part of this root development phase is the wait. Without digging up our seedling, it's almost impossible to know whether any growth is taking place or not. It requires patience. It requires continued discipline of nourishing our seed and maintaining a low compaction of our soil so that our seed has the time needed to begin to grow a strong root system.

It's during this waiting season that we must remain faithful to continue to do the work we began. This is not a passive season, but a very active one.

A farmer who's taken the time to till the soil and plant the seeds doesn't walk away and forget about his young crop hoping they survive. Instead, he's diligent about watering them, checking the environmental conditions so that the seeds have what they need to develop a strong, healthy root system which will be necessary to yield the crop he's expecting. The farmer isn't praying that God grow seeds he never planted and worked to cultivate. Instead, once the farmer has done the labor of cultivating the soil, planting the seeds, watering and consistently feeding the seedling does he trust and patiently wait for God to do what he cannot. The farmer cannot physically make the seed germinate, but God can. The farmer cannot physically make the seed produce a harvest, but God can.

If you want to walk in your calling, then you must plant yourself into the word of God and allow HIM to grow your seed. It takes 9 months of continual growth before a baby is born. It takes 20-30 years of continual growth before a single acorn will develop an oak tree capable of growing more acorns.

It is because God cares SO much about our heart and our character that he gifts us with the privilege of time to develop our roots first. God knows that the journey ahead will be a difficult one. That we will face periods of storms and drought and difficult days. God knows that it will require our roots to be entrenched in him for us to survive, much less thrive, during these seasons. God knows that anything less would cause us to falter and not produce the harvest that awaits.

The harvest each seed will produce is determined while it's still buried and growing its roots in the dark. It is here, in the darkness, that the light of God's word will draw your seed out of the ground to grow towards *THE* light. It is *because* God knows that difficult days are ahead, he requires we first grow our roots deep into him so that we can withstand the drought and hardships that will await.

Points to Ponder:

- How do these verses give me confidence that God IS at work even when I don't see it? Psalm 32:7, Psalm 27: 5, Psalm 31: 20.
- If you're currently in a season of wait, growing your roots in Christ, what are 3 things you can do now which will help develop your root system?
- Finish this sentence, when I'm inpatient I…. what are you telling God about your faith in him when you do this?

Life as a Mustard Seed
Day 7: Seeking God's Voice

The number one thing you can do, each day, is to SEEK God. Seek HIS will for your life. Seek WHAT he would have you do. Seek WHERE He would have you serve. Seek what he would have you CULL from your life. God has given each of us a calling to serve him. The greatest act of obedience that will nourish our seed and promote healthy roots is to stay in his word and to wait on HIM. It doesn't happen overnight, but we WILL see growth in our life and become more receptive to the message he will give us.

Revisiting our planting and farmer analogy from earlier, it is God who is our 'farmer.' He is the one who planted the seed in you. He is the one who knows what 'kind' of seed you are. He is the one who knows the perfect soil for your growth and exactly how much and what kind of food you need to grow the best. He is the one who can survey your spiritual soil and guide the tiller as you cull out the weeds of your life. He is the one who knows Satan's specific herbicide which can kill or weaken your seed.

It is only through TRUSTING in the wisdom of our 'farmer' can we grow and produce the harvest we were created to produce. As the seed, we have no ability on our own to make our roots grow or to force fruit to appear on our branches. BUT, if we stay connected to the 'farmer' by SEEKING HIM and TRUSTING HIS process, then our seed will NATURALLY grow strong, healthy roots and produce fruit.

- If you want to know who you were created to be, SEEK Him.
- If you have questions and need answers, SEEK Him.
- If you want to know where you should go or work or serve, SEEK Him.
- If you want to know what HIS plan is for you, SEEK Him.
- If you want to know how to have a life of impact and significance, SEEK Him.
- If you don't know which way to go, SEEK Him.

There is ONE thing you can do which will completely change the direction of your life and that of your future harvest. It is to, daily, SEEK Him.

As you end this devotional, I pray it opens your eyes, like it did mine to how God works. From personal experience, I can promise you that God WANTS you to uncover your seed. He WANTS you to know and understand him in a very real and tangible way. Regardless of the mistakes you've made, regardless of what has happened to you, God *STILL* has a **GOOD** plan for your life if you will SEEK Him and allow him to direct your steps.

Points to Ponder:

- God promises that if we seek him, we will find him. How do these verses reassure you in your walk? Deuteronomy 4:29-30, Jeremiah 29:12-14, John 10:27
- As you seek him, how can you apply the advice in Psalm 16:7?

Notes:

Day 5
1. Levi Lusko, *Through the Eyes of a Lion,* 139-154

If you liked this devotional, please check out the rest of the *Growing Your Roots for a Mission Driven Life* series!

Next in the series, *Planted in Good Soil* coming out **SPRING 2018**! Check out our website for more resources:

www.rootedleaders.org

Made in the USA
San Bernardino, CA
30 January 2018